Parental Mandate - Speak the Word

We have a responsibility as parents to nurture and pray for our children. In order to point them to Jesus Christ we must be a reflection of God; for the most part Christian parents understand this concept. The overlooked component is teaching our children not only the blessings, benefits and provisions of God but their responsibilities as Christians. They must seek God for themselves, learn the Word of God, reflect God in their character, decisions and conduct in order for them to cultivate their own relationship with God.

Our children live in a world that has a faster pace and rhythm than we experienced and therefore must be trained and equipped.

Know this: Nothing is more powerful than God. Nothing is impossible to God. We have the victory in Christ. We are more than conquerors in Christ Jesus.

God is our Hightower, He teaches our hands to fight (**Psalm 144**). Through prayer we have access to wisdom, knowledge and discernment. Your relationship with God gives you access to the purpose for which your child was created and a map that will give you specific guidance to ensure your child(ren) reaches his/her God given purpose and destiny.

Serving God is in essence a matter of the heart. What you truly feel, think, and understand are beliefs stored in your heart. What you have been taught, your experiences, family and culture help formulate those beliefs. Your beliefs dictate who you associate with, standards, values and most important how you see yourself.

I implore you to take some time before entering this next level and sit at the feet of God. Ask God to show you, you. Allow God into the depths of your heart. As God reveals, ask God to tear down every lie and stronghold that is not of Him. Seek God to build every area of your life, that you and your children walk into a wide path filled with every good and perfect gift.

I pray you move into an intimate place with God where clarity, revelation, wisdom, knowledge, peace, power, authority, blessings, benefits and wholeness abide.

Make room for the abundance God has for you.

Let's go...

Prayer:

May you operate in the fullness of God, you and your children; **In Jesus name I pray, Amen."**

Corinthians 3:17 Now the Lord is that Spirit: and where the Spirit of the Lord is, there is liberty.

Prayer:

Lord show me how to operate in the liberty of the Spirit, help me continuously seek Your guidance on behalf of my child, that he/she grow, learn and flourish in the liberty of God; and with wisdom, fulfill, understand and move toward the calling You Lord God have on his/her life; **In Jesus name I pray, Amen.**"

John 14-26-27 But the Comforter, which is the Holy Ghost, whom the Father will send in my name, he shall teach you all things, and bring all things to your remembrance, whatsoever I have said unto you. 27) Peace I leave with you, my peace I give unto you: not as the world giveth, give I unto you. Let not your heart be troubled, neither let it be afraid.

Jesus said Holy Ghost sent to you by the Father, shall teach you all things and bring all things to your remembrance, whatever Jesus has said to you. No guess work, no worry, no fear because we have Holy Spirit sent by God teaching and speaking everything Jesus says. Thank God for Holy Spirit; continuous intersession, wisdom, power and perfect peace that comes directly from Jesus Christ

Prayer:

"Lord help every parent in the body of Christ intercede and seek You continuously on behalf of their children. Show me everything I need to know and help me place full confidence in Your perfect peace to guide every decision that affects my children according to Your will. May every God-fearing parent known and understand Your Power and Authority. I pray every parent who is willing to turn their face toward You and seek You alone would receive with wisdom, peace that our hearts be not troubled and supernatural revelation to operate at a level the enemy cannot imagine; **In Jesus name I pray, Amen."**

Matthew 12::25 And Jesus knew their thoughts, and said unto them, Every kingdom divided against itself is brought to desolation; and every city or house divided against itself shall not stand:

Every marriage and family in the body of Christ has the responsibility to operate according to God's Word. Our homes shall operate on one accord and our children will see and experience firsthand unity in Christ. Make an intentional decision to stand firm in your marriage (household) and family to endure and thrive in all seasons, do things God's way and your children will follow.

Prayer:

"Lord I seek You to guide me and my house to operate according to Your will and Word. I pray my home be conducive for You to rest, rule and reign. Lord may Your angels encamp about us and watch over our going out and coming in to keep us from all harm both now and forever (*Psalm 121*); In Jesus name I pray, Amen."

I Corinthians 1:10 Now I beseech you, brethren, by the name of our Lord Jesus Christ, that ye all speak the same thing, and that there be no divisions among you: but that ye be perfectly joined together in the same mind and in the same judgment.

Strive to get along and be that example for your children.

Prayer:

"Lord help me always be a godly example for my children. I pray that my _____(child's name) model this example. Lord thank You that _____(child's name) never be unequally yoked with friends, mate, business partner, roommate, spouse or anyone not consistent with faith in Jesus Christ (*2 Corinthians 6:14*); **In Jesus name I pray, Amen.**"

1 Thessalonians 5:23 And the very God of peace sanctify you wholly; and I pray God your whole spirit and soul and body be preserved blameless unto the coming of our LORD Jesus Christ.

Think about the whole child (mind, body and spirit) and what they need to reach their destiny. Seek, pray, fast, teach, labor for your child to live in abundance, wisdom, wholeness, peace, power and glory, exactly the way God intends.

Prayer:

"Lord sanctify _____(child's name), spirit, mind and body in Your truth (*John 17:17*). Teach me I pray to cover, teach and point my child(ren) in the way he/she should go. Thank You Lord _____(child's name) remains safe in Your fortified tower (*Proverbs 18:10*); **In Jesus name I pray, Amen.**"

Amos 3:3 Can two walk together, except they be agreed?

You must be an intentional, purposeful example of living faithful, in complete dependence on God. Maintain open dialogue to make sure your children understand "why" they should be selective and prayerful about friendships/relationships, their conversations and actions, and what they watch and hear. Listen to your children to make sure they understand what God would have them know and do. Don't be afraid to step in when God shows you danger in certain friendships and behaviors. Teaching them along the way is your responsibility.

Prayer:

"Lord I pray _____(child's name) receive Your love that surpasses knowledge, that he/she may be filled to the measure of all the fullness of God (*Ephesians 3:19*), walk in the knowledge of Christ and look to God in every decision. I pray my child(ren) operate with spiritual wisdom and understanding as he/she navigates with purpose throughout life. Thank You Lord for guiding me in parenting Your child; **In Jesus name I pray, Amen.**"

Ephesians 1:3 Blessed be the God and Father of our Lord Jesus Christ, who has blessed us in Christ with every spiritual blessing in heavenly places in Christ:

God has blessed us in Christ with every spiritual blessing in heavenly places. When we understand what God has for us, we are equipped to move into positions of power and authority as God intended. Some things are not going to move until you speak in the name of Jesus who has all power and authority. Ask God to show you the gifts and calling of your children and guide you to strategically place them in fertile holy ground. Praise God for all He has done, is doing and will do.

Prayer:

"Thank You, Christ dwells in our hearts by faith, we are rooted and established in love....I pray my child(ren) grasp how wide and long and high and deep the love of Christ and know His love that surpasses knowledge. My child(ren) are filled beyond measure with all the fullness of God (*Ephesians 3:17-19*). Lord give us clear revelation of your Word to understand and walk in every spiritual blessing, me and my children...to the glory God; **In Jesus name I pray, Amen.**"

Psalm 144: 1-2 Blessed be the LORD my strength, which teacheth my hands to war, and my fingers to fight: 2) My goodness, and my fortress; my high tower, and my deliverer; my shield, and He in whom I trust; who subdueth my people under me.

Parents/grandparent it is your responsibility to be an example; following and serving the Lord, making sure your home has a conducive atmosphere that welcomes the Presence and Peace of God.

Prayer:

"Lord, help me live in transparency when it comes to worship, service, guidance and love of God in my life and home. Help me to seek You, fight spiritually from heavenly places in complete trust and victory in Jesus Christ. Lord I pray _____ (child's name) understand You are his strength who teaches him the responsibilities and service (work) which children of God reflect in order to draw all men to Christ. Lord, You are _____(child's name) goodness, fortress, high tower, deliverer shield, may he/she trust You all they days of his/her life; **In Jesus name I pray, Amen.**"

Ephesians 6:10 - 18 Finally, my brethren, be strong in the Lord, and in the power of His might. 11) Put on the whole armour of God, that ye may be able to stand against the wiles of the devil. 12) For we wrestle not against flesh and blood, but against principalities, against powers, against rulers of darkness of this world, against spiritual wickedness in high places. 13) Wherefore take unto you the whole armour of God, that ye may be able to withstand in the evil day, and having done all, to stand. 14) Stand therefore, having your loins girt about with truth, and having on the breastplate of righteousness; 15) And your feet shod with the preparation of the gospel of peace; 16) Above all, taking the shield of faith, wherewith ye shall be able to quench all the fiery darts of the wicked. 17) And take the helmet of salvation, and the sword of the Spirit, which is the word of God: 18) Praying always with all prayer and supplication in the Spirit, and watching thereunto will all perseverance and supplication for all saints;

vs. 18 Fight your battles in prayer and supplication.

Prayer:

"Lord, I pray my children are covered with the whole armour of God:

- ❖ Breastplate: God's righteousness covers and protects us.
- ❖ Feet shod with preparation of the gospel of peace- I declare my children walk in love, wisdom and knowledge of God.
- ❖ Shield of faith- BELIEVE, speak, pray, meditate and obey the Word of God that defeats and renders powerless the lies and plans of the enemy.
- ❖ Helmet of Salvation - We are saved because of Who's we are and victorious because of what we know; we are redeemed, set free by the Blood of the Lamb. I pray my children believe and meditate to receive the Word of GOD.
- ❖ Sword of the Spirit- Lord we know the Word of God is powerful. We defeat the enemy by standing on the Word that is sharper and any two-edged sword (*Hebrews 4:12*).

I delcare the whole armour of God for my children each and everyday; **In Jesus name I pray, Amen.**"

Colossians 3:21 Fathers, provoke not your children to anger, lest they be discouraged.

It is crucial to teach your children who they are in Christ. Your children can reach their destiny when they understand this. God has given specific instruction for fathers not to provoke children so they will not be discouraged or overwhelmed.

Prayer:

"Lord I thank You for guiding me how to raise the children You have entrusted to me. Help me Lord to nurture, discipline, teach, train and guide _____(child's name) the way You have ordained. Guide my hands, heart and prayers to protect, position and point my child(ren) toward You and the purpose in which You created him/her; **In Jesus name I pray, Amen.**"

Psalm 115:14 The LORD shall increase you more and more, you and your children.

Prayer:

"Lord I thank You for increase in me and my children. Your Word says You will look on us with favor and make us fruitful, increase our numbers and keep Your covenant with us (*Leviticus 26:9*). I pray _____(child's name) relationship with You be pure, progressive, honorable and fruitful; **In Jesus name I pray, Amen.**"

Proverbs 1:33 but whoever listens to me will dwell secure and will be at ease, without dread of disaster.

Prayer:

"Lord, help me listen and obey You that my children and I dwell secure without dread of disaster. I trust You Lord to keep my children in your perfect promise of safety and ease; **In Jesus name I pray, Amen.**"

Job 5:17 Behold, happy is the man whom God correcteth: therefore despise not thou the chastening of the Almighty:

It can be difficult to receive discipline at any age but every parent should understand discipline is necessary and loving. Invite God into every aspect of parenting.

Prayer:

"Lord teach and guide me each day to effectively parent _____(child's name). I pray You would continuously equip _____(child's name) to understand he/she is blessed when God corrects (and chastens) him/her to operate effectively in the kingdom of God (*Job 5:17*). I pray my children and I are joyful in the Lord and remain rooted and grounded in Your Word. I trust in You, LORD and I say, "You are our God." (*Psalm 31:14*); **In Jesus name I pray, Amen.**"

Philippians 4:6-7 Be careful for nothing; but in every thing by prayer and supplication with thanksgiving let your request be made known to God. 7) And the peace of God, which passeth all understanding, shall keep your hearts and minds through Christ Jesus.

God wants to be involved in every area of our lives; mind, body and soul. Pray about every decision, every choice, everything! If you seek God in every area you set the course for your child(ren) to understand who they are in Christ, reach their destiny and fulfill their purpose.

Prayer:

"Lord thank You for knowledge and revelation which derives from prayer and relationship with You. Help my children and I to seek You in all things. I pray that my children abide in Your peace that passeth all understanding and keeps their hearts and minds through Christ Jesus (*Philippians 4:7*); **In Jesus name I pray, Amen.**"

Psalm 94:19 When the cares of my heart are many, your consolations cheer my soul.

Prayer:

"Lord, I submit myself to Your will and pray You teach my children to rest in Christ Jesus. Help us cast all anxiety upon You that worry and fear never be a part of our lives. I pray You sustain my child(ren) and they will never be shaken (*Psalm 55:22*). Thank You for bestowing on _____(child's name) a crown of beauty, oil of joy, a garment of praise and he/she shall be called an oak of righteousness planted by God for His splendor (*Isaiah 61:3*). May our trust, hope and joy always rest in You; **In Jesus name I pray, Amen.**"

Psalm 94:24 But the LORD has become my stronghold, and my God the rock of my refuge.

When you operate according to the things of God and stay in his will, the enemy has no control, no authority, no power over you and your family. God is all powerful. He is your stronghold.

Prayer:

"Lord thank You for being our Stronghold, Rock, Refuge, Protector and Father. Reveal to _____(child's name) who he/she is in Christ Jesus and keep him/her in Your refuge and safety. I pray _____(child's name) operate mightily in all things, according to Your power at work within him/her (*Ephesian 3:20*); **In Jesus name I pray, Amen.**"

Romans 8:32 He that spared not his own Son, but delivered him up for us all, how shall He not with Him also freely give us all things.

May you and your children always understand how much God loves each of you. If God willingly sent His son as Savior, He will surely give us freely a good and abundant life filled with purpose and power.

Prayer:

"Lord, I declare on behalf of _____(child's name) You are the horn of his/her salvation, rock, refuge and stronghold. Help my child(ren) understand and receive the love, purpose, power, favor and grace You have given him/her. I pray _____(child's name) always define himself/herself as a child of God and walk out his/her salvation in powerful revelation and knowledge; **In Jesus name I pray, Amen.**"

Psalm 145:8 The LORD is gracious, and full of compassion; slow to anger, and of great mercy.

Prayer:

"Lord I thank You for compassion and grace. I pray in the name of Jesus _____(child's name) receive with understanding Your grace, compassion and love for him/her. Lord, help me to demonstrate Your love to ____(child's name) in every aspect of parenting. I pray my children grow strong in the Lord, to live their lives in Your light; the seed of the righteous shall be delivered (*Proverbs 11:21*); **In Jesus name I pray, Amen.**"

Psalm 115:15 Ye are blessed of the LORD which made heaven and earth.

All blessings come from God.

Prayer:

"My house is blessed of the LORD. Thank You for granting my child(ren) unending blessings and making them glad with the joy of Your Presence (*Psalm 21:6*). I pray me and my children acknowledge all blessings come from You Lord Jesus. Our God is Omnipotent, Omnipresent, Omniscient, Holy and worthy of all our honor and praise; **In Jesus name I pray, Amen.**"

Isaiah 54: 13-15 And all thy children shall be taught of the LORD; and great shall be the peace of thy children. 14) In righteousness shalt thou be established: thou shalt be far from oppression; for thou shalt not fear; and from terror; for it shall not come near thee. 15) Behold, they shall surely gather together, but not by Me: whosoever shall gather together against thee shall fall for thy sake.

God has given you His Word to protect His children.

Prayer:

"Lord I thank You for teaching _____(child's name) in all things. Thank You Lord, my children are in peace with You, established in Your righteousness, far from oppression, fear and terror.
_____(child's name) is enthroned in Your presence forever and You have appointed Your love and faithfulness to protect him/her (*Psalm 61:7*); **In Jesus name I pray, Amen.**"

Isaiah 54:17 No weapon that is formed against thee shall prosper; and every tongue that shall rise against thee in judgment thou shalt condemn. This is the heritage of the servants of the LORD, and their righteousness is of Me, saith the LORD.

Without question or doubt God is more than willing and fully capable to fulfill His Word. **Isaiah 55:11** "So shall My Word be that goeth forth out of My mouth: it shall not return unto Me void, but it shall accomplish that which I please, and it shall prosper in the thing whereto I sent it."

Prayer:

"I declare the Word of God; the enemy is incapable to form a weapon against me or my children that can prosper. We condemn every tongue that would speak against us in judgment. We are triumphant, righteous, secure; this our heritage in the LORD; **In Jesus name I pray, Amen.**"

Psalm 143:9-12 Deliver me, O Lord, from mine enemies: I flee unto thee to hide me. 10) Teach me to do thy will: for thou art my God: thy spirit is good; lead me into the land of uprightness. 11) Quicken me, O Lord, for thy name's sake bring my soul out of trouble. 12) And of thy mercy cut off mine enemies, and destroy all them that afflict my soul: I am thy servant.

God protects His children. Jesus prayed to the Father in *John 17:12* "While I was with them, I kept them in your name, which you have given me. I have guarded them, and not one of them has been lost except the son of destruction, that the scripture might be fulfilled."

Prayer:

"Lord, teach us of Thy great power, for Your name sake deliver me (and my children) (our souls) out of trouble. Have mercy on us and cut off every enemy and destroy them that afflict our souls. We take refuge in You Father. I pray Lord lead us to the land of uprightness for we are your servants; **In Jesus name I pray, Amen.**"

Zechariah 3:2 And the LORD said unto Satan, The LORD rebuke thee, O Satan; even the LORD that hath chosen Jerusalem rebuke thee: is not this a brand plucked out of the fire?

Jesus told his disciples "I saw Satan fall like lighting from heaven" (**Luke 10:18**). The only way the enemy is a threat to the children of God is if you step outside the will of God. Our God has plucked him from the fire.

Prayer:

"Lord I thank You for defeating and rebuking the enemy protecting my children and I from all hurt harm and danger. May we always remain in Your refuge. You have given us the victory through our Lord Jesus Christ (*1 Corinthians 15:17*). We stand on the Word of the LORD, Satan the LORD, my Father rebuke thee; **In Jesus name I pray, Amen.**"

Psalm 144:11 Rid me, and deliver me from the hand of strange children, whose mouth speaketh vanity, and their right hand is a hand of falsehood.

Parents it is imperative you set yourselves apart from the things of the world. Priority is a must; God first, family, body....mirror God's order.

Prayer:

"Lord I pray my children worship You and You would deliver them from the hand of all their enemies (*2 Kings 17:39*). I pray _____(child's name) operate in Your wisdom and refuge in such a way he will recognize and reject anything that does not line up with Your will for his/her life. I declare in the name of Jesus worldly enticements will not appeal to my children but instead _____child's name remain true and faithful to the things of God. May each and every child remain forever firm in Your righteousness, protection, peace and perfect will; **In Jesus name I pray, Amen.**"

Colossians 1:9-14 For this cause we also, since the day we heard it, do not cease to pray for you, and to desire that ye might be filled with the knowledge of His will in all wisdom and spiritual understanding; 10) That ye might walk worthy of the Lord unto all pleasing, being fruitful in every good work, and increasing in the knowledge of God; 11) Strengthened with all might, according to his glorious power, unto all patience and longsuffering with joyfulness; 12) Giving thanks unto the Father, which hath made us meet to be partakers of the inheritance of the saints in light: 13) Who hath delivered us from the power of darkness and hath translated us into the kingdom of His dear Son: 14) In whom we have redemption through His blood, even the forgiveness of sins.

Parents be intentional, diligent and continuous in prayer for your children.

Prayer:

"Lord I thank You. You have delivered my children and I from the power of darkness, making darkness powerless to us. May _____(child's name) be filled with the knowledge of Your wisdom and spiritual understanding according to Your Power. Help us Lord walk worthy unto You always fruitful in every good work, ever increasing in knowledge of God, strengthened in Your might. Thank You Lord for making us meet to take part in the inheritance of the saints; **In Jesus name I pray, Amen.**"

Hebrews 2:17-18 Wherefore in all things it behoved Him to be made like unto his bretheren, that He might be a merciful and faithful High Priest in things pertaining to God, to make reconciliation for the sins of the people. 18) For in that He himself hath suffered being tempted, He is able to succor them that are tempted.

Jesus the Son of God in mercy and love was made like us to pay for our sins. Jesus was tempted in every way, just as we are, yet He did not sin (*Hebrews 4:18*).

Prayer:

"Lord thank You for Your mercy, love, grace and salvation. I pray no temptation overtake us. God is faithful; You will not let us be tempted beyond what we can bear. But when we are tempted, You provide a way out so that we can endure (*1 Corinthians 10:13*). In the name of Jesus we are victorious in Your will. Lord, You alone are our rock and our salvation, You are our defense and we shall not be moved (*Psalm 62:6*); **In Jesus name I pray, Amen.**"

Psalm 115:15 You who fear the LORD, trust the LORD! He is their help and their shield. 12) The LORD has remembered us; He will bless us;......13) He will bless those who fear the LORD, both the small and great. 14) May the LORD give you increase, you and your children 15) May you be blessed by the LORD, who made heaven and earth.

Such is the favor and blessings of our LORD.

Prayer:

"My children are like olive trees flourishing in the house of God; I trust in God's unfailing love forever and ever (*Psalm 52:8*). I pray for spiritual eyes and ears to receive and walk in the peace and blessings You have for us. Thank You for giving us increase, me and my children; **In Jesus name I pray, Amen.**"

James 5:16 Confess your trespasses to one another, and pray for one another, that you may be healed. The effective fervent prayer of the righteous man avails much.

Proverbs 27:17 tells us "...iron sharpens iron..". Prayer is one of the most powerful tools we have. Prayer literally changes the atmosphere and reaches heavenly heights.

Prayer:

"Lord look upon us in mercy and hear our prayers and petitions...(*Daniel 9:17*). You are our refuge, habitation and deliverance. You have set Your love upon my children and commanded Your angels to watch over them (*Psalm 91:11 &14*) Fulfill Your purpose in _____(child's name) keeping him/her in Your perfect will. I plead the Blood of Jesus over my children to abide in Your protection, peace, wisdom, glory and truth. May he/she serve You all the days of his/her life. By day the LORD directs His love, at night His song is with us -- a prayer to the God of my life (*Psalm 42:8*); **In Jesus name, Amen.**"

Hosea 4:6 My people are destroyed for lack of knowledge; because you have rejected knowledge, I reject you from being a priest to me. And since you have forgotten the law of your God, I also will forget your children.

This is a powerful verse that teaches us the importance of attainting and walking in the knowledge and will of God. You are responsible and expected to serve God as a priest. If you do not the consequences not only separate you from God but God will forget your children.

Prayer:

"Lord I seek from this day forward to attain and walk in Your knowledge. I pray that my children serve You alone all the days of their lives. Father I pray wisdom enter the hearts of my children and knowledge always pleasant to their souls (*Proverbs 2:10*). I declare my children maintain discretion and preserve knowledge (*Proverbs 5:2*). LORD God help my children have great success, victory and do all that you have put in their hearts to do; **In Jesus name I pray, Amen.**"

James 2:13 For judgment is without mercy to one who has shown no mercy. Mercy triumphs over judgment.

May we as parents receive and experience God's mercy and extend that mercy to our children.

Prayer:

"Lord I thank You for mercy on behalf of my children which means freedom from the judgment of people. I pray my children always walk in Your love, forgiveness and freedom. I declare my children will never be judged, punished or mistreated because the color of their skin, gender or any other worldly standard and opinion. I pray we will have a boldness to proclaim Jesus to all people. May the way we serve our fellowman represent Your love and lead others to Jesus Christ our Savior; **In Jesus name I pray, Amen.**"

Jeremiah 29:11 For I know the thoughts I think toward you, saith the LORD, thoughts of peace, and not of evil, to give you an expected end.

Prayer:

"Our God is with us; my children will not fear because God strengthens and helps them. Your righteous right hand of justice, power, victory and salvation hold my children (*Isaiah 41:10*). I pray Your wisdom and understanding of the gifts You have placed in _____(child's name). Guide me in education, extra-curricular activities, friends, sports, college, dating and every decision involving my children. Show me all that I need to know as I seek You on behalf of them. I pray my children and I receive Your perfect peace and expected end; **In Jesus name I pray, Amen.**"

Isaiah 59:21 As for me, this is my covenant with them, saith the LORD; My spirit that is upon thee, and my words which I have put in thy mouth, shall not depart out of thy mouth, nor out of the mouth of thy seed, nor out of the mouth of thy seed's seed saith the LORD, from henceforth and for ever.

Prayer:

"God Almighty, our hope, strength and trust are in You. Your Word says, "The righteous lead blameless lives; blessed are their children after them" (*Proverbs 20:7*). I stand on Your righteousness this day and proclaim my children blessed beyond measure. May I always be aware of the responsibility, benefits, wisdom, peace, power and authority of the covenant I have with You. Your Spirit dwells within us, as we operate, speak and live in victory according to and in alignment with Your covenant; standing on Your Word that my children and grandchildren shall remain in this same covenant, a lasting legacy of dedicated love and service to our Father; **In Jesus name I pray, Amen.**"

1 King 19:11-12 And He said, go forth, and stand upon the mount before the LORD, and behold the LORD passed by, and a great and strong wind rent the mountains, and break in pieces the rocks before the LORD; but the LORD was not in the wind: and after the wind and earthquake; but the LORD was not in the earthquake: 12) and after the earthquake a fire; but the LORD was not in the fire: and after the fire a still small voice.

Help my children look to You and listen in complete obedience to Your voice.

Prayer:

"Lord I know if my children seek You with all their heart and soul, they shall find You and call upon You in ever season (**Deuteronomy 4:29**) I pray _____(child's name) know Your voice and will not follow another and because my children know You they are strong and do great exploits (**Daniel 11:32b**). Some trust in chariots, and some in horses: but we will remember the name of the LORD our God (**Psalm 27:7**). I pray my children trust in You LORD God all the days of their lives and hearken to You above all others; **In Jesus name I pray, Amen.**"

Job 10:12 Thou hast granted me life and favour, and thy visitation hath preserved my spirit.

Prayer:

"Lord I thank You for life and favor. Help my children and I to speak and expect Your favor to go before us as a shield. Since we live by the Spirit, let us keep in step with the Spirit (*Galatians 5:25*). I declare my children will live in hope, favor, victory and joy every second of every day as You give us fresh revelation of all You would have us know and do. I pray we acknowledge You alone for all that we are; **In Jesus name I pray, Amen.**"

Thank your LORD that the battle is not ours but Yours (2 Chronicles 20:15).

Psalm 119:165 Great peace have those who love thy law; nothing can make them stumble.

Prayer:

"God of hope fill my children with all joy and peace in believing, that they abound in hope, in the power of the Holy Spirit (*Romans 15:13*). Father, I pray grace and peace be multiplied to _____(child's name) as You guide him/her: mind, body and soul to be obedient, disciplined and purposeful in the things of God. I pray _____(child's name) forever love You Lord and nothing can make him/her stumble; **In Jesus name I pray, Amen.**"

Hebrews 4:12 For the Word of God is quick, and powerful, and sharper than any twoedged sword, piercing even to the dividing asunder of soul and spirit, and of joints and marrow, and is a discerner of the thoughts and intents of the heart.

God is going to perform His Word. There is nothing more powerful neither can anything escape or hide from God's Word. The Word of God can discern the intents of the heart and give you revelation of everything you need to know.

Prayer:

"Lord thank You for Your Word that reveals to us all truth in the natural and spiritual realm. On behalf of _____(child's name) I declare supernatural revelation and discernment. I pray that as _____(child's name) trusts You, rivers of living water will flow from within him/her (*John 7:38*). Lord show _____(child's name) everything You need him/her to know, guide his/her prayers, thoughts, desires and actions to align with Your will; **In Jesus name I pray, Amen.**"

Psalm 144:12-15 That our sons may be as plants grown up in their youth; that our daughters may be as corner stones, polished after the similitude of a palace: 13) That our garners may be full, affording all manner of store: that our sheep may bring forth thousands and ten thousands in our streets: 14) That our oxen may be strong to labour; that there be no breaking in, nor going out; that there be no complaining in our streets. 15) Happy is that people, that is in such a case: yea happy is that people, whose God is the LORD.

Prayer:

"Lord I thank You my sons are blessed in their youth as You have spoken. My daughters are royalty shaped by the breath of God. Thank You for giving us harvest, blessing and increase for our house. The work of our hands always brings forth abundance, our businesses bring thousands and ten thousands without mishap, loss, failure or distress. Thank You for Your abundant blessings. Our God is LORD; **In Jesus name I pray, Amen."**

Jude 1:20-21 But ye, beloved, building up yourselves on your most holy faith, praying in the Holy Ghost 21) Keep yourselves in the love of God, looking for the mercy of our Lord Jesus Christ unto eternal life.

Prayer:

"I pray my children have faith in God (*Mark 11:22b*). May the grace of our Lord Jesus Christ, and the love of God, and fellowship with the Holy Spirit be with _____(child's name) (*2 Corinthians 13:14*). God of peace, sanctify us (my family and I) completely. May our whole spirit, soul and body be kept blameless at the coming of our Lord Jesus Christ (*1 Thessalonians 5:23*). We humbly remain forever blessed by our LORD.; **In Jesus name I pray, Amen.**"

Philippians 1:6 Being confident of this very thing, that He which hath begun a good work in you will perform it until the day of Jesus Christ.

God expects His children to have complete confidence in Him and His Word, to trust and seek Him always. This has to be intentional and genuine. Your actions, decisions and obedience are outward evidences of trust, service and love for God.

Prayer:

"Lord may _____(child's name) always see himself/herself as You see him/her. I declare _____(child's name) heed to instruction, prosper and be blessed because he/she trust in You, LORD (*Proverbs 16:20*). I pray Father order my child's steps and help him/her know and understand he/she was created for a purpose that fulfills the desires of his/her heart. May _____(child's name) never believe a lie but trust with full confidence in You alone; **In Jesus name I pray, Amen.**"

1 Peter 1:3 Blessed be the God and Father of our Lord Jesus Christ! According to his great mercy, he has caused us to be born again to a living hope through the resurrection of Jesus Christ from the dead.

Prayer:

"Lord, Your Word says; I will be his Father, and he shall be my son: and I will not take my mercy away from him...(*1 Chronicles 17:13*). Jesus' great mercy has given us everlasting life, hope, peace, power, love from God our Father. Blessed be Your glorious name and may it be exalted above all blessing and praise (*Nehemiah 9:5b*). Thank You for being a good God whose mercy endureth forever (*1 Chronicles 16:34*); In Jesus name I pray, Amen."

Philippians 3:14 I press toward the mark for the prize of the high calling of God in Christ Jesus.

This verse should help you and your children stay grounded with the understanding of pressing (working) toward the high call God has on your lives.

Prayer:

"To the only wise God our Savior, be glory, majesty, dominion and power both now and forever; I declare Your clarity, wisdom and vision for _____(child's name) to press toward the mark of the high call of God, that he/she would cleave to You and understand You have chosen and appointed him/her with purpose to bear fruit that remains (*John 15:15*); **In Jesus name I pray, Amen.**"

Jeremiah 17:7 Blessed is the man who trusts in the LORD whose trust is the LORD.

Trusting God and doing what is right is not always easy or popular. This can be difficult as an adult and more so for our children. God tells us in His Word, you will be blessed when you trust in the LORD.

Prayer:

"Lord I trust You and believe Your way is best for me and my family. I pray _____(child's name) seek the kingdom of God and Your righteousness with all his/her heart and soul (*Matthew 6:33*); In Jesus name I pray, Amen."

Philippians 4:9 Those things, which ye have both learned, and received, and heard, and seen in me, do: and the God of peace shall be with you.

Prayer:

"My children are rooted and built up, strengthened and taught by You Lord God and overflowing with thankfulness (*Colossians 2:7*). Lord hide Your Word in _____(child's name) heart that he/she be a reflection of what Your love and wisdom accomplishes is him/her; **In Jesus name I pray, Amen.**"

Isaiah 60:1 Arise, shine; for thy light is come, and the glory of the LORD is risen upon thee.

Don't allow the world, society or peers to define your child's breath and worth. We are what God says we are; a wonderful creation in Jesus Christ. Where there is light, darkness cannot exist.

Prayer:

"Lord I declare my children walk in the knowledge; they are chosen by God, created for a purpose and destined for greatness. I pray You keep my children in the light and glory of Your presence; **In Jesus name I pray, Amen.**"

Deuteronomy 29:29 The secret things belong unto the LORD our God: but those things which are revealed belong unto us and to our children for ever, that we may do all the words of this law.

God loves you and your children which makes you important to the kingdom.

Prayer:

"God has saved us and called us to a holy life....because of His own purpose and grace given to us before the beginning of time (**2 *Timothy* 1:9**). I pray my children love You Lord with all their heart, soul and mind and love their neighbor as themselves doing all that You have ordained and purposed (***Matthew 22:37-39***). Show me the call You have on the lives of my children and help ____(child's name) to understand who he/she is in Christ Jesus. May we abide in Your love forever; **In Jesus name I pray, Amen.**"

Isaiah 53:5 But He was wounded for our transgressions, He was bruised for our iniquities: the chastisement of our peace upon him; and with his stripes we were healed.

Confirm this in your spirit daily. Listen for Gods' voice continually, hear God guide your every decision and turn. Jesus took the punishment that resulted from our sins and iniquity and in turn gave us his peace and divine health.

Prayer:

"Lord may we forever abide in Your will. I pray _____(child's name) have ears to hear Your voice and a heart that seeks to follow in complete obedience. Lord Jesus, You were wounded for our transgressions, bruised for our iniquities, given us Your peace and healed us from everything past, present and future because of this my children will never walk in condemnation or bondage in any area; mind, body, or spirit. Lord help us to receive these blessings always; **In Jesus name I pray, Amen.**"

Proverbs 3:26 for the LORD will be your confidence and will keep your foot from being caught.

Dialogue with your children and help them understand how to put their trust in God. Make sure they understand why they trust God so they can be prayerful, mindful and purposeful.

Prayer:

"Lord I place complete confidence You protect and preserve my children who are counted as blessed in the land, shielded from every enemy (*Psalm 41:2*). Thank You for keeping _____(child's name) firm to the end, safe in Your will, blessings and purpose, blameless and beyond reproach in the day of our Lord Jesus Christ(*1 Corinthians 1:8*); In Jesus name I pray, Amen."

Colossians 4:6 Let your speech be always with grace, seasoned with salt, that ye may know how ye ought to answer every man.

Friendly reminder - be careful what you say.

Prayer:

"Jesus, I seek to honor You. Help me speak in love and wisdom being mindful of the power of my words at all times and to all people. I pray _____(child's name) understand the power of his/her words and his/her speech be grace filled, seasoned with the Word of God and he/she will know how to answer every man; **In Jesus name I pray, Amen.**"

Psalm 121 I will lift up mine eyes unto the hills, from whence cometh my help. 2) My help cometh from the LORD, which made heaven and earth. 3) He will not suffer thy foot to be moved: he that keepeth thee will not slumber. 4) Behold, he that keepeth Israel shall not slumber nor sleep. 5) The LORD is thy keeper: the LORD is thy shade upon thy right hand. 6) The sun shall not smite thee by day, nor the moon by night. 7) The LORD shall preserve thee from all evil: he shall preserve thy soul. 8) The LORD shall preserve thy going out and coming in from this time forth, and even for evermore.

Speak, declare and decree God's Word over your life and the lives of your children.

Prayer:

"Lord I look to You as our Source and help. I pray my children remain rooted and grounded in Jesus. Our (my children and I) help comes from our LORD, Creator of heaven and earth. God will keep us on solid ground. The LORD is our provider and protector, shield and buckler; night and day. The LORD preserves my children and I from all evil, He preserves our souls this day and forevermore; **In Jesus name I pray, Amen.**"

Romans 5:5 And hope maketh not ashamed; because the love of God is shed abroad in our hearts by the Holy Ghost which is given unto us.

Prayer:

"Lord thank You; the Holy Ghost reveals Your love, wisdom and grace. May the God of hope fill _____(child's name) with all joy and peace as he/she trust in You and overflow with hope by the power of the Holy Spirit (*Romans 14:17*); **In Jesus name I pray, Amen.**"

1 Thessalonians 5:21-22 but test everything; hold fast what is good. 22) Abstain from every form of evil.

Be an example; consider the things you say and do and strive to serve God.

Prayer:

"Thank You Father, when You breathed life into _____(child's name) You also breathed destiny, purpose and power. My children are planted in Your house, shall flourish like palm trees and grow like cedars in Lebanon; they shall flourish in Your courts and still bear fruit in old age, staying fresh and green proclaiming the Lord is upright, He is our Rock and there is no unrighteousness in Him. (*Psalm 92:12-15*) I pray _____(child's name) hold fast to what is good, abstain from every form of evil and seek You above all to honor and obey You with all his/her might. God of Peace sanctify my children through and through. May their whole spirit, soul and body be kept blameless at the coming of our Lord Jesus Christ (*1 Thessalonians 5:23*); **In Jesus name I pray, Amen.**"

The Journey Continues

Everything you need to know about parenting is found in God and His Word. The Bible is the living Word which contains our history and future. It takes faith in Christ Jesus to take up the mantle, serve God and do his will no matter what. The benefits far exceed the sacrifice. Work hard, commit, cling to, and love God; dig into the Word, square your shoulders, expect, prepare, speak, think and declare God's will be done in your life and the lives of your children.

Children of God operate and live from a different realm of power, peace and wholeness. God wants us to live our lives and raise our children to be salt of the world.

Prayer:

"God show us how to be godly parents, examples and reflection of You. Jesus is Lord; we are honored to serve; **In Jesus name I pray, Amen.**"

Names of God

YHWH/YAHEH/JEHOVAH: LORD, the revelation of the name is first given to Moses " I AM who I AM" Exodus 3:14. Power and Authority.

EL, ELOAH : God - Mighty, Strong, Prominent

ELOHIM: God - Creator, Mighty and Strong

EL SHADDAI: God Almighty

ADONAI : Lord

YAHWEH-JIREH: The Lord Will Provide

YAHWEH-RAPHA: The Lord Who Heals

YAHWEH-NISSI: The Lord Our Banner

YAHWEH-M'KADDESH: The Lord Who Sanctifies

YAHWEH-SHALOM: The Lord Our Peace

YAHWEH-ELOHIM: LORD God

YAHWEH-TSIDKENU: The Lord Our Righteousness

YAHWEH-ROHI: The Lord Our Shepherd

YAHWEH-SHAMMAH: The Lord Is There

YAHWEH-SABBAOTH: The Lord Of Hosts

EL ELYON: Most High God

EL ROI: God Of Seeing

EL-OLAM—Everlasting Go